Seaside Summer

BY BRIAN ROCKVAM

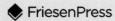 FriesenPress

Suite 300 - 990 Fort St
Victoria, BC, V8V 3K2
Canada

www.friesenpress.com

Additional Contributers:
Emily Bourke (Illustrator)
Hillary Rockvam (Editor)

ISBN
978-1-5255-5728-6 (Hardcover)
978-1-5255-5729-3 (Paperback)
978-1-5255-5730-9 (eBook)

1. POETRY, SUBJECTS & THEMES, PLACES

Distributed to the trade by The Ingram Book Company

I dedicate this book to my grandmother, Sandra Clarke, without whom I wouldn't have had the opportunity to spend a good portion of my childhood summers at my favourite BC island, a place where I have formed lifelong memories and friendships. It is truly my happy place.

An old school bike
is what I like

to ride from place to place.

On Sports Day
we like to say,

Tubing lots,
oops, I forgot,

jumping off
the dock.

Spotting deer
without a fear

and large bald
eagle flocks.

Boating trips

and salty lips

from swimming in the sea.

Big
salmon
fishing

then shooting-star wishing
creating smiles of glee.

A game of cards

and beach
glass shards
while lounging
on the shore.

Stress-less days
in countless bays.

You couldn't ask
for more.

Hot chocolate cups.

And grey seal pups floating in the water.

Breaching whales,
slimy fish tails.

Oh, look! There's an otter!

Marshmallow roasting
and crab-trap boasting
while sitting by the fire.

A Monopoly game,

it's never lame;
the fun level
only gets higher.

Swimming shorts
and tennis courts;
you'll never want
to go.

Wonderful friends,
the fun never ends.

You'll have to visit to know.

About the Author

Brian is a young BC author who has had a passion for writing since a young age. Having spent a month or more of every summer of his life with his family at his at grandmother's summer cottage on the west coast of Canada, at the age of 17 he felt compelled to write a poem about many of the childhood summertime activities which he loves so much. 8 years later his fond memories are being brought to life for all to enjoy.